E-Learning in the Classroom

E-Learning in the Classroom
By Dr Alan Clarke

First Published in 2009 by Lulu

ISBN 978-1-4092-9448-1

Acknowledgements

The author and publisher wishes to acknowledge and thank the following for use screen captured images as illustrations within the book: Microsoft and Google.

Microsoft product screenshots reprinted with permission from Microsoft Corporation

Google product screenshots reprinted with permission from Google

Microsoft and Google trademarks are acknowledged

Every effort was made to trace the copyright holders and obtain their permission for the use of copyright material. The publisher and author will gladly receive any information enabling them to rectify any error or omissionin subsequent editions.

Contents

Introduction

This is the first in a series of books aimed at helping tutors develop their professional practice in e-learning. E-learning is a rapidly developing field, so practiitioners must continuously improve their knowledge and skills. These books concentrate on specific areas of e-learning and combine theory with practice so that you can develop a sound professional approach.

This publication is focused on using e-learning in face-to-face situations such as in the classroom or lecture theatre. However, it also includes approaches that integrate classroom practice with online learning. It will consider how e-learning can enhance learning and improve the effectiveness of teaching. Many of the approaches are often termed, blended learning which involves integrating and combining conventional approaches with technology.

The book includes sections on sources of information and tools which are intended to help you take forward the ideas discussed in the book. There are many website addresses given but because the web is dynamic it is likely that some will have changed by the time you read this book.

Chapters are provided on competency and on how to keep up-to-date. These are important in a volatile and dynamic subject such as e-learning.

There are various names for practitioners in post-school education (e.g. teachers, lecturers, tutors, trainers, instructors and faculty) throughout the book the term tutor will mainly be used to cover all the terms and situations.

E-learning is difficult to define in a clear concise way since it is a mixture of approaches, technologies and methods. However, a clear definition was provided by Hertfordshire University's Blended Learning Unit at a JISC Learning and Teaching Practice Expert Group meeting on 9th July, 2008. It was:

"Enhancing learning, teaching and assessment through harnessing technology"

Chapter 1

E-learning principles, theory and practice

It is important to consider what learning theory tells us about effective practice so we can make choices that will enhance learning. This is true in almost any learning context but especially so in relation to using information and communication technology (ICT). ICT is often associated with hype and the considerable pressure to employ the latest developments in your teaching. There are always going to be new developments but each needs to be assessed for its suitability and appropriateness. In many cases straightforward applications can produce real benefits. The key is linking the needs of the learners to the possibilities that technology can provide.

Constructivist

This book is not concerned with explaining theories but rather looking at what they can tell us about practice. Learning theories can help us realise how to create the most effective learning environment. Constructivism is often linked to e-learning. It suggests that learning takes place when people are:

- active learners

- able to relate the new knowledge and experience to their prior learning

- able to construct new knowledge from the learning experience

- free to collaborate with other

- considering open questions

- creating outcomes

- Assessed through portfolios of evidence

- Discovering new relationships and concepts

This suggests that an effective constructivist learning environment would provide learners with opportunities to solve problems, build on their existing skills, work together in groups and be actively involved. The tutor's role in this type of environment would be more facilitator, moderator, mentor and coach rather than the traditional tutor standing at the front of the class lecturing.

Each of these roles overlaps to some extent so precise definitions are difficult to arrive at, but some general ones are given below:

- facilitators are concerned with creating a learning environment in which they support and aid learners by offering guidance (e.g. suggesting approaches to address a task), acting as a resource and encouraging a learner-centred approach.

- moderator's role is often associated with online forums and other features in which the learners interact with each other. The moderator assists, encourages and referees the interaction so that everyone is helped to participate within agreed boundaries.

- mentors provide access to an experienced person who can advise and discuss issues that concern the individual. They are often a person with considerably more experience of the individuals' work or background and who understands their perceptive.

- coaches are concerned with improving the performance of an individual by carefully reflecting with them on their efforts, offering focused guidance on developing specific aspects of their achievements

The role that you may follow will often combine several aspects.

Instruction

Hartley (1998) listed some principles for instruction based on cognitive psychology. They are that:

- instruction should be well-organised.

- instruction should be clearly structured.

- the perceptual features of the task are important. Learners need to have the problem or objective of the learning presented to them in a meaningful way, using language and context appropriate to them.

- prior knowledge is important. It is essential that new content clearly relates to and builds on earlier learning.

- differences between individuals are important as they will affect learning.

- cognitive feedback gives information to learners about their success or failure concerning the task at hand.

Hartley (1998) stressed that understanding must be at the centre of instruction. It is not sufficient that learners are able to recount facts; they must understand their relevance and context.

Integration

If we combine instructional principles with the constructivist environment then structure, planning and organisation are also needed to create an effective learning climate. This requires considerable effort. Simply providing everyone with a computer and a problem to solve is not sufficient.

The constructivist approach is more suitable when you are trying to develop higher level skills such as working with others, problem solving techniques and trying to motivate individuals and groups. Instructional methods are often more appropriate when developing foundation skills and helping to develop practical skills. In straightforward terms, instruction is more about traditional methods such as the worksheet while constructivist approaches are more concern with groups working and studying wider questions. E-learning can be applied in both contexts to design better materials or facilitate wide ranging discussion and investigation.

The instructional approach is appropriate to the development of e-learning materials. By contrast, constructivism is more suitable for social networking methods (e.g. blogs, wikis, e-portfolios, webquests and discussion forums).

Reflection

A key element in learning is reflection. The principles of instruction emphasise building on earlier learning and understanding whereas constructivism is concerned with individuals constructing their own knowledge. All these factors are assisted by the opportunity and willingness to reflect on learning experiences. There is a range of theories about reflection. Kolb (1984) offers a cyclical model of reflection (figure 1). This proposes that reflection occurs after an experience and leads to the formulation of ideas and theories that need to be tried and tested. This in turn results in more experience and reflection and so on. It suggests that it is important for tutors to allow the learners opportunities to reflect on experiences and to encourage them to act on any conclusions formed during reflection.

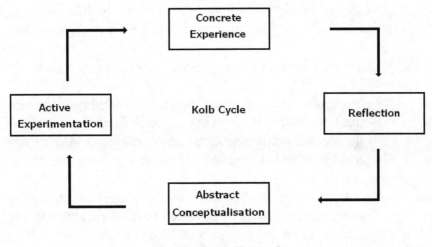

Figure 1 *Kolb Cycle*

Reflection is the systematic review of the learning experience. It involves:

- observation – considering and describing the learning experience to clarify the key points in relation to the individual's needs

- analysis – analysing the experience to identify what are the key factors

- insight – considering what it means to the individual

- context – considering the learner's context

- improvement – comparing the relationship with existing knowledge and skills and identifying changes to improve performance

The process of reflection is critical in turning surface or superficial learning experiences into deep and meaningful learning. It does not matter whether the learning approach is instructional or constructivist. Reflection needs to be integrated into the process.

E-learning offers several ways of supporting reflection such as:

- blogging – the individual blog can be used as a learning diary in which the individuals can reflect on and review their learning experiences. It has the considerable advantage that the other learners can add comments to the blog.

- learning diary – the individuals can keep an electronic learning diary that is a reflection of their learning but which is not limited to text. It can incorporate still or moving images and also sound.

- group reflection –by using an electronic voting system, groups can reflect on their experiences.

Knowledge, Skills and Attitudes

A straightforward way of considering education or training is in terms of three factors:

- Knowledge – are you trying to improve the learners knowledge of the subject?

- Skills – are you trying to improve the learners' skills?

- Attitudes – are you trying to change the learners' attitudes?

You may well be seeking a combination of all of these factors. E-learning can assist with all three in many ways such as:

- using the wealth of information on the World Wide Web to develop knowledge

- employing video and still cameras to capture evidence of skills development or offer feedback to the individual

- technology to motivate groups to work together

There are many ways that e-learning can contribute. These are just three examples.

Combination

When preparing for a course or a specific session consider your objective and how it relates to instruction or constructivism, how best to encourage reflection and which factors it is helping to develop. Table 1 provides some examples.

Summary

The key points of this chapter are:

- consider your aims and objectives in relation to the learning theory

- ensure there are opportunities and encouragement for learners to reflect

- use technology appropriately to meet your learners' needs

Table 1 Approach and Objective

Objective	Practice and Theory	Reflection	Notes
Basic Skills - literacy	Instruction	Self - assessment (e.g. a quiz)	Individuals can study at their own pace Mainly knowledge with some skills
Problem solving	Constructivist	Provide time for personal review of what each person has learned	Group work Often an excellent way of changing attitudes
Motivation	Constructivist	Personal electronic learning diary	Some form of creative activity is often motivating and can help an individual develop knowledge, skills and change attitudes
Collaboration	Constructivist	Personal learning diary to which other members of the group can contribute (e.g. a blog)	Collaboration can be a powerful way of changing attitudes but can also contribute to developing knowledge and skills
Practising skills	Instruction	Viewing a video of the practice can provide stimulus for reflection	Practice is essential for skills development

Chapter 2

Benefits and limits of
e-learning approaches

Many studies of e-learning have sought to identify the benefits that technology can bring to learning. They cover learners over a wide range of ages but many have focused on children while others have been concerned with cost savings in training situations. It is easy to dismiss many of them as inappropriate but almost all have something useful to say about the effectiveness of e-learning. E-learning is a global phenomenon so that research undertaken in North America, Asia, Europe or Australia can be a source of important insights.

When judging the appropriateness of evidence to your own teaching or training you should consider:

- Who were the research subjects (e.g. age and gender)?

- How large was the study (e.g. large is not always beautiful but small may be unconvincing)?

- What were they learning (e.g. specific subjects may have their own pedagogical approach)?

- How was the technology employed?

- What was the context (e.g. school, workplace, college or university)?

- Tutors' technology and e-learning expertise (i.e. staff skills are frequently an initial component)

- Learners' technological and learning expertise (i.e. without the most appropriate skills learners are not able to benefit from e-learning)

These questions will help you decide if the outcomes of the research could be transferred to your context. Furthermore, considering the use of e-learning in different contexts can be a source of new ideas and challenges to your existing practice.

Some of the main benefits that e-learning has brought to learning are:

- raising standards (Becta, 2007)

- enhancing learners' employability (Becta, 2007)

- improving motivation (Becta, 2007)

- impovingtutors'productivity(Becta,2007;Northumberia University, 2008)

- improving achievement and retention rates (ALI, 2007; Northumberia University, 2008)

- helping learners present their work (ALI, 2007)

- encouraging people to take up learning (ALI, 2007)

- improving ICT skills through e-learning (ALI, 2007)

- helping to develop positive attitudes to learning, building confidence and encouraging people to return to learning (ALI, 2007, Hall Aitkin, 2002; Clarke et al, 2003; Northumbria University, 2008)

- supporting learners with learning difficulties and disabilities (Northumberia University, 2008)

- offering learning on a 'just in time' basis provides continuous access to education, training and information (CIPD, 2006)

- providing uniformity of delivery of training (CIPD, 2006)

- achieving cost reductions (CIPD, 2006; Northumberia University, 2008)

- reducing the time it takes to deliver training (CIPD, 2006)

- logging or tracking learning activities (CIPD, 2006)

- ability to personalise the training for each learner (CIPD, 2006)

Many e-learning investigations have concluded that benefits would only be realised by careful planning, adequate resources and focused activity. It is perfectly possible to gain the interest and engagement of a group of learners through a small development such as using digital cameras within a project but on its own it is unlikely to gain the larger benefits. These require a more systematic, significant and embedded approach.

It is useful to compare these results with the views of practitioners. At a workshop, tutors identified the following benefits:

- open access to learning and resources

- instant feedback and results

- flexibility

- discovery-based learning – e-learning enables learners to find information online and apply their acquired knowledge

- creating a collaborative learning community

- creating new and interesting learning activities

- giving learners more control over their own learning

- e-learning makes tutors challenge their assumptions about the teaching methods they use

The other key issue is to employ e-learning in an appropriate and relevant way to the subject being studied and the learners involved. Some examples of appropriate use are:

- capturing evidence with a digital camera of a physical activity or outcome for a portfolio

- using a word processor to encourage learners to edit their work to improve presentation, grammar and spelling

- using an electronic quiz to allow learners to self-assess

- developing a pod cast as a group to assist with the development of speaking and listening skills

- using computer-based simulations to investigate hazardous environments

- communicating with students through text messages about administrative matters (e.g. the assignment is due on Thursday)

- motivating a group through the use of video technology

The key to appropriate use is that e-learning is being used for a purpose that relates to the learning objective and the learners' context.

Poor Practice

All learning, teaching and training methods can be used badly and e-learning is not an exception. Some examples of poor practice are:

- learners presenting a scrap book of text and pictures cut and pasted from websites without any analysis or originality

- learners being unaware of the objective of the e-learning activity

- unstructured searching of the World Wide Web

- failure to integrate the e-learning into the course

- using technology as a gimmick

- converting classroom activities into e-learning without considering the differences in media

Summary

The key points of this chapter are that:

- e-learning is a dynamic, evolving subject so it is important to consider relevant research

- challenging your own views and experience through considering practice from different contexts can be valuable

- planning, resources and focused activity are vital to successful e-learning implementation

- it is important to relate the use of e-learning to the subject being studied and the learners' needs

- e-learning is not a universal panacea and can be poorly used

Chapter 3

Motivating learners

Several studies, reports and investigations have shown a relationship between the use of e-learning and learner motivation. This is not simply that a computer or other technology will act like a magic wand but when technology is used effectively, as an aid to learning, it can motivate people. With learners who are returning to education or training after a long break and who perhaps had a poor initial experience, technology is often very motivating. This is perhaps because technology is not associated with past poor experiences and also that ICT may have high status with these learners. It is also obvious to many people that ICT skills are now essential in gaining and retaining employment.

E-learning can be employed in many different ways. It can assist:

- individuals (e.g. allowing them to work at their own pace)

- learners working in pairs (e.g. help collaboration)

- small groups (e.g. enable everyone to contribute to the group task)

- a whole class (e.g. create an engaging climate)

E-learning allows individual learners to work at their own pace through interacting with learning materials that let them study, practice, self assess and have a personalised learning experience. However, it would be poor practice to spend every session with the whole class working individually. It is important to maintain a balance of activities, providing individual support and not simply relying on material.

Learning in pairs is often effective in that it provides peer support and encourages a co-operative and collaborative approach. The key is to ensure that the pair is not dominated by one individual or that it becomes two individuals working independently next to each other. It is important to select an activity that needs input from both learners such as using a video camera to record each person's feedback with their colleague acting as the camera operator.

Small group working (i.e. less than six) has been widely used in education and training for many types of learning. It is again important to establish roles whereby everyone can participate. Consider the group task and select one that needs everyone to contribute. Communication technology allows groups to continue to communicate between sessions and that may be an important factor. Groups need support so tutors need to review progress regularly and offer assistance if needed. There is a need to balance individual freedom to choose when to participate with the groups need to complete the task on time.

Whole class approaches using technologies such as voting systems and electronic whiteboards can create exciting, creative and engaging atmospheres. There is also potential to combine small groups, pairs and individual activities together. An example would be to ask groups of learners to prepare a presentation and the use the electronic whiteboard to present it to the whole class. Voting systems would allow individuals to participate perhaps by selecting answers to a question and then explaining why they chose a particular answer.

Motivation can be achieved when e-learning is used:

- effectively and appropriately – incompetent application of e-learning is not going to motive anyone

- to challenge learners

- to make them question their understanding

- to allow them to participate (e.g. using an electronic whiteboard to present their conclusions)

- to provide more choice (e.g. learners like choice but remember that making the best choices requires good understanding and a learner may not always be well placed to make them)

Overcoming Barriers

ICT can prove an important means to remove barriers and obstacles that face disabled learners. The Adult Learning Inspectorate (2007) identified that e-learning was a key benefit for disabled learners and those with communication problems.

Accessibility is vital and there are a large number of alternatives to standard equipment available, as well as operating systems that allow computer systems to be adjusted to meet individual needs. Often tutors are not aware of alternatives or adjustments and need to take advice. Techdis (http://www.techdis.ac.uk/) and Abilitynet (http://www.abilitynet.org.uk/) are services which provide advice. There are many straightforward actions that you can take to assist your disabled learners. Appendix 3 offers information about how to use the functions within Microsoft Windows to make it more accessible.

Feedback

Learners will always seek feedback since without it they can become disillusioned and de-motivated. Technology offers many ways of enhancing feedback such as:

- e-mail and other online communications – many learners find it difficult to ask questions in a face-to-face group. E-mail offers the means of sending questions directly to the tutor for a personal response. Tutors can provide feedback in the one-to-one setting that e-mail provides. It allows learners and tutors to question and discuss issues.

- electronic assignments can be annotated using comments and track changes functions. This enables detailed feedback to be given.

- conferences and forums – online groups can discuss and debate issues between face-to-face sessions so that peer feedback and support can be provided without the restriction of waiting until everyone is physically present.

- e-learning content often has feedback embedded into its design (e.g. take a test and receive a response).

- digital cameras can capture learners' efforts to undertake skilled activities. This can be used to give accurate feedback to them (e.g. coaching in sport, showing how an individual asks questions and providing the means to help people improve their use of tools).

Multimedia

Learners have preferences for different types of approaches to learning. E-learning allows the use of a richer mix of media (e.g. sound, images and video) so that it can meet their needs. It also provides opportunities for interesting alternatives to the printed handout or textbook.

Multimedia is often identified for presenting information but it is probably just as important in providing a focus for a learner's project or assignment. A powerful force for motivating learners is developing multimedia as part of a project. It can bring a group together or offer an individual the opportunity to be creative.

Example
Create a podcast to explain a concept
Produce a video to demonstrate a set of skills
Design a presentation to illustrate the outcomes of a project

Learners' expectations

Learners live in a busy, intense world in which there are many demands on their time and distractions from study. This puts a premium on maximising their choice and the flexibility of learning delivery so that it can be integrated into their lives. People own lots of technology (e.g. mobile telephones, MP3 players, PDAs, DVD players and computers). They are comfortable users of their own equipment (JISC, 2007) so if it is possible to use it for learning, it is more likely to be successful than if they have to learn how to use new hardware.

It is widely accepted that the World Wide Web is the most used source of information for learners. However, success clearly depends on the learners' ability to judge the appropriateness and quality of information as well as on their search skills. Tutors will often need to assist learners to improve their information skills in both searching and judging the quality of information. There is evidence that learners are not highly skilled in searching for and judging information but tend to rely on the top hits of search engines.

The first generation of learners who have grown up with technology as a normal part of their lives are now entering post compulsory education. They are at least going to expect that ICT will form part of their courses and that the technology in use in schools will be available in college. Often people have access to considerable amounts of technology (e.g. MP3 players, smart phones, laptops and digital cameras) and this provides opportunities for learning that should not be ignored. However, it is not clear that they are always willing to use their personal social networking sites for their education and training or that they have the learning skills to take advantage of e-learning. They may wish to differentiate their personal and learner lives from each other.

It is likely that these younger learners will be able to:

- word-process assignments

- use the Internet to locate sources of information

- access course materials online

- be taught in classrooms with electronic whiteboards

- communicate with tutors and peers through e-mail and other technologies

- use their personal equipment (e.g. laptops and PDAs) to help with their studies

There is evidence that some disadvantaged young people do not have the technical skills and access to technology expected of the rest of their generation. It is also important to realise that e-learning is not solely dependent on technical skills but also requires the appropriate learning skills. It is probable that many students will need help to develop their learning/study skills.

Successful e-learners (Clarke, 2008) are likely to be:

- self-confident

- positive to their learning

- motivated

- effective communicators

- able to work collaboratively and co-operatively

- competent and confident users of ICT

Only one aspect of this list relates directly to technology. It is therefore important when designing e-learning activities to recognise the importance of helping students develop their learning skills. It is good practice to integrate opportunities to develop the learner's skills within the course activities.

Seventy percent of the people who will be in employment in 2020 are already in the UK workforce. This means that many learners are not graduates of the technology generation and their skills and expectations will be different? It is widely accepted that many adults with a previous poor experience of education are keen to learn with and through technology. They clearly see e-learning as not being linked to their previous poor experience and thus as a new opportunity. Their motivation is probably also related to improving those ICT skills which are now essential for finding and retaining employment.

While learning skills are important to these older learners, it may be many years since they took part in education and training so their study skills may be poor. Knowles (1983) reported some assumptions of the nature of adult learning. They are:

- adults need to know the reason for learning before they begin to study

- adults are responsible for their own lives and thus their learning

- adults have a lifetime of experience with which to enrich their learning

- adults are motivated to learn when they have a need

In terms of e-learning, adult learners require that the aims and objectives of the learning are made clear and its relevance demonstrated to them. This can be further extended to explaining why they are using technology if the subject being studied does not involve ICT. Adults accept ownership for their learning so potentially may benefit more from those e-learning techniques that encourage them to take responsibility, such as online discussion groups.

Information Literacy

The enormous information resource provided by the Internet and other e-learning approaches cannot be fully exploited by an individual with no information literacy skills. These skills have been defined in a variety of ways but tend to emphasise factors such as:

- searching skills to locate information on the World Wide Web and individual websites

- judgement of the quality of information (e.g. is it valid?)

- identifying bias within the presentation of the information

These skills are essential to become effective e-learners in the information age and it is therefore good practice to try to develop them within e-learning activities.

Examples

Groups of learners are asked to consider the information presented on a range of websites concerning a topic they are studying and to judge which site most influences them and why.

Learners are asked to search the web to locate sources of information about a problem then list them in order of usefulness, giving their reasons for their judgement

E-learning Learning Skills

The importance of "learning to learn" has been widely emphasised. E-learning re-emphasises this need since it provides new and different approaches to becoming a competent learner. Technical skills are often identified and are clearly important, but there are further additional learning skills or changes in emphasis.

Traditional learning tends to be associated with listening (e.g. a lecture) and speaking (e.g. answering questions) whereas online learning requires a greater focus on reading and writing (e.g. short e-mail messages). This is a change in emphasis since while traditional learning skills also identify reading and writing, it is not normally a short message contributing to a discussion. Online reading is often called browsing and it involves the skills of navigation. Reading a book has similarities (e.g. links through content pages and the index) but there are obvious differences in presentation and length.

E-learning offers more freedom of choice to learners but with freedom comes the need for acceptance of responsibility and time management. Often those e-learning courses that maximise choice are also accompanied by poor retention rates because learners are not skilled at managing themselves and their learning.

It is essential to develop these skills and this can be achieved by integrating them into activities.

Examples

Within each group task, appoint a leader who has the role of ensuring the group finish on time.

Ask people to analyse the contributions to a discussion in order to produce a guide for future participants on effective practice.

Summary

The key points of this chapter are that:

- e-learning can be employed in many different ways (e.g. individual learners, groups or the whole class)

- e-learning can motivate when used effectively and appropriately to challenge learners, encourage them to participate and offer them more choice

- barriers to learning can be overcome (e.g. place, pace, time and disability)

- feedback is enhanced by e-learning through the use of communication technology, annotation of electronic assignments, online forums and using cameras to give visual comments

- using and creating multimedia can enrich learning

- different groups of learners will have varying expectations (e.g. young learners expect to have access to and be using technology in their education and training)

- technical skills are not sufficient for e-learning - they must be accompanied by e-learning (study) skills

- information literacy is essential to exploit the potential of the World Wide Web

Chapter 4

Creating effective e-learning opportunities

Introduction

Technology has been used in education and training for more than two decades, although the term 'e-learning' is more recent. In the past, terms such as computer-assisted learning, computer-based training, flexible learning and technology-based learning have been used. Technology is now applied to almost every subject, with ICT essentially providing a set of tools that can be used in any way that seems appropriate, meeting or contributing to the meeting of a learning need. Table 2 gives some examples of technologies satisfying a need.

Table 2 Technology Examples

Examples	
E-learning - Technology	**Learning Needs**
1. Digital camera	Capture evidence for an assessment portfolio Develop learning resources Illustrate a project report Provide a focus for an individual or group project

(Continue)

Examples	
E-learning - Technology	**Learning Needs**
2. Video camera	Provide feedback on a physical activity or skill (e.g. construction) Develop learning resources Provide a focus for an individual or group project
3. Word processing	Presentation of assignment Edit documents Spelling, grammar and thesaurus tools Proofreading Group activity (e.g. create a joint document using the track changes function in the word processor)
4. Spreadsheet	Model mathematical information Presentation (charts and graphs)
5. Simulation	Science techniques and methods
6. Digital sound recording	Interviews Record impressions during a field trip
7. World Wide Web	Information source for almost any subject Focus for projects Media literacy Information literacy
8. Virtual learning environment	Electronic handouts Administration information Course and assessment information Communication Discussion forums

(Continue)

Examples	
E-learning - Technology	**Learning Needs**
10. Blog	Learning diary – reflection Discussion
11. Data logging	Science experiments
12. Control technology	Engineering, electronics and science

Tutors have always designed learning activities. Technology provides a far greater and richer range of possibilities (JISC, 2004) through the range of tools available to tutors (e.g. Microsoft PowerPoint presentation, spreadsheet quiz and using Exe to create learning materials). Table 3 provides some examples of teaching and learning activities and how technology can enrich them.

Table 3 Teaching and Learning Examples

Teaching and learning	Technology	Advantages
Presentation	Electronic Whiteboard Video Projector Microsoft PowerPoint	Focusing learners attention Using multimedia to motivate Providing notes and handouts Easy to revise material
Handouts	Word processing Desktop Publishing Image editors	Producing a quality product Easily up-dated Distribute on college VLE

(Continued)

Feedback Formative assessment	Camera Annotation of electronic assignments Quiz Voting system	Visual feedback for skills Immediate feedback Comparison with peers Assists discussion
Collaborative working	Wiki Google Docs Track Changes in Microsoft Word	Allows groups to work on a joint project asynchronously Jointly write and edit a report
Support	E-mail Text message Instant Messaging Skype	Allows support outside of face-to-face sessions
Reinforcement	Interactive materials	Allows for individual practice to reinforce learning
Course materials	Virtual Learning Environment (VLE)	Materials always available Easy to up date
Submission of assignments	E-mail attachment	Efficient and helpful to part- time and disabled students who do not need to travel to college to submit

Learning Strategies

JISC (2007) provided a summary of effective learning strategies in a digital age. The list below is based on this publication.

Effective learning strategies include:

- blending learners' personal technology with college education approaches, both traditional and technology based

- supporting reflective learning through technology (e.g. blogs)

- using technology to provide flexible provision (e.g. freedom to study when, where and at your own pace)

- online communities to provide peer support

- using a wide range of communication technologies to maintain and develop relationships

- providing multimedia content

- using accessible technology to overcome the barriers that disabled learners encounter

- creating content

Twigg (2005) reported on a national programme in the USA to redesign whole courses using e-learning methods. The subsequent evaluations of the new programmes demonstrated improved retention and achievement combined with cost savings. Some of the lessons that the programme demonstrated are:

1. Large results are a by-product of redesigning significant elements rather than making small changes

2. The redesign needs to focus on making the course more learner-centred

3. E-learning resources can play a key role in encouraging participation

4. It is critical to provide support when the learner needs it

Creating Materials

A powerful approach is the employment of ICT to enable learners to create content. This can be either simple or complex. A group could be asked to investigate an issue and then produce a presentation or a poster. This is a familiar learning task. The technology provides the tools so that the activity is enhanced and the learners motivated. Other possibilities of the approach can include creating:

- a webpage

- an electronic handout for future learners of the course

- a film of an event and editing it

- a podcast

- a slide show

Many learners find creating material exciting and motivating and it can be the means of helping them to develop:

- team working

- communication skills

- design skills

- research skills

It is an effective way of learning and can be applied to almost every subject. The content can be used as evidence to be included in a portfolio for the course assessment.

Materials created by one course can often assist another group of learners by providing examples of what can be achieved.

Communication

Communication technology can extend classroom activities so that a face-to-face discussion can continue in the course e-mail forum without the need to wait until the next session.

Online discussion forums provide the opportunity to encourage participation from quiet students. Everyone is equal online and no one can block a contribution or hog the conversation. Achieving the best results requires careful moderation and agreed rules (i.e. netiquette). An effective initial exercise is to ask the group to agree the netiquette for the forum. Some basic netiquette rules are:

- never reply in anger to a message

- always respect the views of others

- don't distribute messages that are not part of forum's objectives

Reflection

Some e-learning approaches are aimed at helping learners reflect on their experiences. This is important since reflection is a way of ensuring that deep rather than surface learning takes place. Using blogs to develop a form of online learning diary in which peers and tutors can send comments is often an effective way of encouraging reflection. The requirement to include reflections of learning activities in e-portfolios is another approach that is often useful. Reflections can form part of e-mail discussion forums or collaborative activities such as wikis.

The differences between surface and deep learning are:

- surface learning
- recall of facts without context

- passive learning (e.g. listen and take notes without questioning the content)

- no understanding of overall picture

- deep learning

- relating facts to existing knowledge

- active participation (e.g. questioning new ideas)

- structuring knowledge and identifying key points

Reflection needs to involve more than simply describing experiences in an individual blog/learning diary. It requires learners to challenge the experience, analyse it in relation to their previous experience and relate it to their existing understanding.

Learners will probably need to practise the skills of reflecting and writing a blog as well as contributing to the blogs of their peers. The comments of other learners are often very useful and encourage learners to reflect on their peers' reflections. Tutors need to support and encourage this process.

Some ways of encouraging and supporting reflecting are:

- offer examples of reflection

- provide guidance on how to reflect

- provide an initial assignment to help practise reflecting

- offer feedback on reflecting

- integrate reflecting into the assessment of the course (i.e. both creating a blog and commenting on peers' reflections)

Focus for projects

ICT can provide an interesting focus for projects and assignments. These are widely used in education and training to enable learners to undertake investigations, write reports, create content and presentations and participate in active learning processes. Technology adds an extra dimension by allowing new activities to be included such as:

- using a video camera to create a multimedia report

- using a wiki to allow the group to write a document collaboratively

- using Microsoft PowerPoint and a digital camera to produce a visual presentation

- using a digital recorder to capture interviews as part of a survey

Technology can often turn a straightforward activity into an exciting and engaging one. It can ensure learners focus on identifying key issues through, say, the need to edit video, to analyse sound recording and to select appropriate still images. Wikis can assist learners develop team working skills. Employers are often critical that young people lack the soft skills of communication, team working and self management. ICT-centred projects offer many opportunities to develop these as well as gaining understanding and skills in relation to the course.

There are numerous ways that technology can be employed; the only limitation is imagination.

World Wide Web

The web has an enormous library of information held on its websites. Ways to exploit it include:

- simply being asked to search for information to support writing an essay or completing an assignment; to make this effective the learners need to be skilled in search techniques and able to judge the quality and appropriateness of information they locate

- providing students with a series of sources for them to locate and use as part of their studies

- webquests in which a group of learners are provided wth a range of website sources of information and asked to undertake a specific task using the information

Learners often have limited search skills and need help to improve them. In a similar way their ability to judge the quality of online information may need to be developed.

Word processing

Word processing is an important tool in education and training since it provides the means of producing well-presented assignments. It does this by providing an efficient means of revising and editing a student's work. With a hand-written report, revision is only possible if the whole document is rewritten, whereas word processing allows for several revisions and checks to be made. Currently, few assignments would be hand-written but that does not mean that the potential of word processing is realised in every case. Many students still do not proofread their work or even use the spelling and grammar checking facilities.

Other students employ the word processor to over- present their work by employing a range of fonts, emboldening text, using italics and general using too many functions. The best assignments are consistent, using features such as underlining to emphasis systematically rather than at random.

Track changer is a useful function, enabling a document to be prepared in collaboration. It allows everyone to see the proposed changes before finalising them. It can also be used during marking to provide feedback to the student. The comments function is also useful in letting you annotate an electronic assignment with feedback.

Spreadsheets

Some courses require learners to manipulate numerical data or to present evidence in a tabular way. Spreadsheets (e.g. Microsoft Excel) provide the means to analyse numerical information and also to present data. Numeric information can also be presented in a variety of charts and graphs, enriching project reports.

Models can be created so that students can explore the question "What if?" with their data. Trends can be considered and the relationship between variables investigated. Spreadsheets offer a wide range of mathematical tools to help undertake numerical analysis.

Databases

Databases are designed to keep records. Possible uses of them in learning include:

- keeping records of references/sources of information

- holding survey data

- holding experimental data

Mind mapping tools

A key factor in many subjects is to recognise and identify the links and relationships between concepts and factors. Mind mapping applications provide a visual means of undertaking the mapping and sharing the results. FreeMind is an open source tool (http://freemind.sourceforge.net/wiki/index.php/Main_Page).

Presentation Applications

There are a number of presentation applications of which Microsoft PowerPoint is probably the best known. Additionally there is PhotoStory for Windows (figure 2), a free Microsoft application aimed at helping users who want to use still images to tell a story. The images can be edited and manipulated in straightforward way.

Figure 2 *PhotoStory for Windows*

Presentation applications can be used to enhance a talk (e.g. reporting on a project) or to create learning materials.

Desktop Publishing

It is normal practice to ask groups and individual students to prepare materials such as posters, leaflets and other publications after researching a subject. The activity provides a focus for the work and provides an alternative outcome from essays or reports. It is also more suitable for group work.

Desktop Publishing applications provide the means to produce high quality products. They can combine digital images that the group or individual learner have taken, with text and graphics they have produced. This can prove a highly motivating experience.

The outcome of desktop publishing should be designed to be used. This is more motivating than an activity simply designed for education and training outcomes.

Example

Create a poster to show the research that the group has undertaken and then display all the posters so that the whole class can benefit from the research.

Create a leaflet to explain the course to new learners.

Create a webpage to present the outcomes of a project.

Online Applications

Office applications are now available online, allowing users to work from anywhere and to share their efforts with other people. These facilities offer the potential for collaborative and co-operative learning. Figure 3 illustrates Google Docs, a set of online office applications and storage.

A class group could employ the storage to create a resource of useful materials as well as for creating content.

Figure 3 *Google Docs*

Mobile learning

The availability of mobile technology that people can carry with them is increasing rapidly. Like other forms of technology, it can be used to assist learning. At the moment the mobile telephone is often greeted in class with the request to switch it off so that its ringing does not distract. However, portable technology needs to be welcomed since it allows learners to study at any time and anywhere. Some examples of the potential of mobile equipment are:

- listening to podcasts as the learner travels in order to maximises study time using an MP3 player

- text messaging – a straightforward way to send reminders or course change information

- capturing evidence of learning or taking a photograph of information displayed on a notice board or whiteboard quickly and easily using a digital camera

- keeping a record of a lecture, interview or sound of an event using a digital sound recorder

- accessing to e-mails, the Internet and applications on the move with a PDA or smart phone

There is considerable interest in mobile learning since the technology has created the potential to turn any location and time into one suitable for study. Many individuals own a range of mobile devices so that it should be a natural step to use them for learning.

Sound

The use of recorded speech to provide tutorial support is not new. The tape and cassette recorder have been extensively used for decades to deliver tutorials at a distance. In many ways a podcast is a similar approach with the big difference that the podcast can be distributed far more widely and easily.

Podcasts can be used for a variety of purposes such as providing:

- additional content to extend or enhance a session

- briefing for a trip, test or practical activities

- advice and guidance about the course (e.g. study guide, aims and objectives and qualifications)

- an alternative means of presenting learning material

- help with revision

The key steps in creating a podcast are to:

- write a script and read out the content very few people can ad-lib an educational podcast

- keep it short or break it into short section so that the learner only has to focus for a few minutes at a time

The technology is widely available and consists of:

- a microphone

- A computer with a sound card and some storage space (most modern equipment)

- Audacity – a free application that will turn your words into a digital format

- An application to turn the audacity files into MP3 format (LAME)

- An MP3 player

Podcasts can be distributed as simple attachments to an e-mail or uploaded onto a site that distributes podcasts or added to the content of your Virtual Learning Environment.

Examples of learning activities

E-learning can be used in a variety of ways. The following are some examples showing the learning objective, approach and technology.

Climate Change	
Objective:	To analyse the evidence for climate change
Approach:	Tutor identifies and bookmarks ten examples of climate change evidence available online Divide class into small groups, pairs or individuals Ask learners to analyse the evidence and write a short article of their reasoned conclusions
Technology:	Websites

Creative Art	
Objective:	To encourage the discuss of art and motivate artists
Approach:	To create an art gallery website and discussion group Artists capture their work using a digital camera and write an introduction to the work that encourages visitors to the site to send comments. Artists respond to comments
Technology:	Digital camera Web editing application Mail group

Analysis	
Objective:	To analyse traffic flow at different times of the day
Approach:	Divide class into small groups
	Ask each group to record the number and type of vehicles using a specific road at different times of the day
	Develop a spreadsheet model that will allow the group to analyse the flow and create charts to present their model
Technology:	Spreadsheet

Information Literacy	
Objective:	To develop the skills to judge the quality of online information
Approach:	Individual learners are asked to evaluate the information published on specific websites and to post their findings in a discussion forum
	Learners are then asked to discuss their different views and how they have been arrived at
Technology:	World Wide Web
	E-mail discussion forum

Health and Safety	
Objective:	To undertake a risk assessment of a workplace To prepare for and carry out an interview with workplace staff
Approach:	Divide class into pairs Ask each pair to assess the health and safety risks of a workplace including interviewing staff and recording their comments with a digital recorder Ask them to record any risks using a digital camera Prepare a multimedia report using sound recording and pictures.
Technology:	Digital sound recorder and camera Presentation software (e.g. Microsoft PowerPoint)

Communication Skills	
Objective:	To develop communication skills
Approach:	Divide class into groups Each group is asked to create a video in relation to the subjects they are studying such as induction to the college for new learners
Technology:	Digital Video

Media Literacy	
Objective:	To consider the way news is presented by different organisations
	To determine what factors influence presentation
Approach:	Divide class into small groups
	Each group is asked to consider a specific news story and how it is presented on a national broadcaster website (e.g. www.bbc.co.uk), a national daily newspaper and a 24 hour news television news station.
	Each group to provide a presentation using the class electronic whiteboard
Technology:	Website and electronic whiteboard

Discussion Skills	
Objective:	To develop learners' ability to discuss a topic with their peers
Approach:	Locate a series of online materials covering a specific topic or news story
	Allocate the resources to individual learners and ask them to read content and reflect on the key points
	Ask learners to discuss the topic or news story with each other
Technology:	World Wide Web

Foreign Language	
Objective:	To develop foreign language conversation and vocabulary
Approach:	To establish a mail group with another group of students in another country
	Encourage discussion through internet telephony, e-mail or other communication methods on shared topics
Technology:	E-mail, VOIP or other communication technologies

Summary

The key points of this chapter are that:

- ICT is essentially a set of tools that can be used in any way that seems appropriate; the key is to meet or contribute to meeting a learning need

- matching the technology to the learning approach and enhance it

- using effective learning strategies (e.g. blending learners' personal technology with college education approaches, support reflective learning through a blog and provide online peer support)

- large effects require significant change (e.g. redesign whole course)

- creating content is an exciting and engaging way to learn

- communication technology can extend classroom activities

- reflection needs to be encouraged so that deep rather than surface learning is achieved

- ICT can provide an interesting focus for projects and assignments

- there are many ways to exploit the enormous library of information that is held on websites (e.g. simply searching, providing sources and webquests)

- mobile learning has the potential to turn any location and time

  into one suitable for study

- applications (e.g. word processing, spreadsheets, databases, presentation tools and online resources) can be used to enhance learning

Chapter 5

E-learning teaching and learning approaches

Introduction

E-learning and technology can be widely used to enhance teaching and learning. It can, for example:

- help the productivity of the tutor (e.g. create high quality worksheets and other learning materials)

- provide a focus for learning activities involving individuals, pairs, small groups and the whole class

- provide learning materials (e.g. interactive courseware and learning objects)

- assist communication whereby the course is not just limited to face-to-face sessions, but discussion and interaction can become continuous

- improve the quality of presentation of portfolio evidence or other assessments

- provide assessments (e.g. quizzes)

- capture evidence (e.g. sound recordings)

At the beginning, it is probably best to select an area that interests you and your learners and develop that approach before expanding into other areas. Many tutors begin with personal productivity producing handouts, lesson plans and other materials. This is fine but you should always strive to move forward and gain all the advantages of e-learning. E-learning is a dynamic subject with new methods and tools continuously becoming available. It is therefore important to consider new methods as part of continuous professional development.

Golden et al (2006) investigated the use of technology in learning by tutors in FE Colleges. They reported that technology was frequently used to:

- prepare for courses (e.g. research and preparing materials)

- present information

It was also used by a minority of tutors for:

- assessment

- personalised learning

- providing individual support

- communication between sessionsV

This suggests that many tutors are still in the early stages of using e-learning.

Show, Tell and Do

Instruction is sometimes categorised as show, tell and do.

- Show – demonstrate the context, reveal the skills or provide examples

- Tell – explain, lecture or discuss the ideas, knowledge and concepts relevant to the subject

- Do – this is usually asking the learners to practise the skills or use the knowledge they have gained from being shown and told

Most teaching or training involves aspects of all three categories. Table 4 shows how technologies can relate to them.

Table 4 Technologies and Show, Tell and Do

Tools	Show	Tell	Do
Electronic Whiteboard	Demonstrate Present examples	Presentation multimedia	Ask learners to use the whiteboard to explain the outcomes of their work
E-mail forums	Offer links to online resources	Provide answers to questions Offer additional briefing Discuss issues	Co-ordinate and collaborate on group projects and tasks
Vodcast/ Podcast	A vodcast incorporates video into the presentation and offers an effective way of showing an event to learners	Listening to a podcast is an alternative way of explaining a topic with the advantage that it can be listened to anywhere	Getting a group of learners to create a podcast can be a motivating way of helping them practise skills, analyse information and also present facts

Memorise, understand and do (MUD)

Another approach to learning can be stylised as memorising, understanding and doing:

- Memorising – this is concerned with recalling the facts

- Understanding – being able to explain the why and the how of an issue or subject

- Do – this relates to the physical movements required in learning skills

Table 5 shows how technologies can relate to MUD

Tools	Memorise	Understand	Do
Presentation of assignments using applications	Often memorising is assisted by producing documents or making notes	Understanding is helped by organising facts into relevant order	Presentation to peers and tutors
Blogs	Posting images and linking to visual resources	This allows the issues to be discussed, compared and contrasted and alternatives debated. This will assist learners to gain an understanding beyond the simple recall of the facts.	Provides peer support for learners' developing skills

(Continued)

Digital video and stills	Visual information is often useful in remembering information	Multimedia can assist with understanding	Video records and still photographs can be useful aids in providing feedback to a learner who is developing physical skills. It can show clearly the positioning of limbs and movements

Good practice in Undergraduate Education

Chickering and Gamsom (1987) offer seven principles on which to base good practice in undergraduate education. The list below is based on their work and is intended to provide a framework or structure to consider the effective use e-learning in education and training. Although the principles were originally intended for higher education they are also appropriate for other forms of post-compulsory education and training.

The seven revised principles are:

1. develop the relationship and communication between learners and tutors

2. encourage collaboration and co-operation between learners

3. provide opportunities for active learning

4. provide feedback on demand

5. assist learners to develop time management skills and ensure adequate time is allowed for activities

6. set high standards

7. flexibility of approaches and acceptance of alternatives

Blending

There are considerable advantages in the blending of e-learning approaches with tradition teaching methods. Essentially you are trying to gain the benefits of both approaches, with perhaps the expectation that the sum would be greater than the parts. Table 6 suggests some links or blends between e-learning and traditional methods

Table 6   Blends

Traditional Methods	E-learning Method	Discussion
Lecture	Electronic Whiteboard Video projector Virtual Learning Environment (VLE) (e.g. storing course notes and handouts) Text message	There are numerous ways that e-learning can assist a lecture, from simply offering electronic copies of handouts to providing effective presentation technologies that engage learners.

Demonstration	Digital video/still images Simulation	Demonstrations can be captured and stored thus enabling learners to review and revise them at a later date. Simulations can bring into the classroom an experience that would otherwise be impossible to provide due to health and safety or practical reasons.
Team teaching	Communication technology	Team teaching requires careful preparation and good communications. E-mail and other communication technologies allow co-ordination to be achieved.
Discussion	E-mail discussion forum Record Blogs	Face-to-face discussions can be enhanced and extended by removing the limitations of time. Online discussions are recorded so that learners can review them to help their revision or simply as an aid to catching up if they have fallen behind (e.g. due to illness).

Test	Quiz Voting systems E-portfolio	Tests can be enhanced by using quizzes so that individuals can self-assess. Voting systems can engage groups and provide a focus for discussion. E-portfolios provide the means of keeping evidence of achievement.
Field trip	Digital video/still images Digital sound recording	Actual experience is a powerful means of learning. Video, still camera and sound recorders offer the means to record the experience for later use. Digital resources can be the focus for a group activity on return to the classroom to maximise the benefits of the trip.
Role play	Webquest Video	Webquest are a way of undertaking an analytical role play task based on the consideration of the information held on selected websites. Role plays in the classroom can be recorded using video or sound devices for analysis and to provide feedback.

Assignment	Content creation (e.g. podcast and presentation) Wiki	Collaborative activities can be based on developing resources or joint activities such as the production of a group document.
Feedback	Comments on blogs E-portfolio comments E-mail discussion forums Annotation of electronic assignments	There are many ways of providing feedback from both the tutor and peers.

Productivity

A tutor's first use of ICT is most likely to be for personal productivity. Office applications are often described as productivity tools. They could be used to:

- word process handouts – this has the benefit of making updates quicker while providing a high quality document

- create spreadsheets – using a spreadsheet to plan a course – this has the added benefit of being able to provide students with a clear plan and also allow a way of coping with any changes

- desktop publish – to produce high quality course materials (e.g. study guide, timetable and brochures)

- develop learning materials (e.g. Microsoft PowerPoint)

- aid evidence collection of physical activities (e.g. digital camera)

- send text messages or e-mails to inform the group of any changes

- manage time (e.g. Microsoft Outlook to assist with self-organisation)

There are no doubts many more examples whereby applications can make a tutor more efficient.
E-learning Classroom

The organisation of the e-learning classroom needs to be carefully considered. The stereotype computer room is often designed to allow for individual use but without considering peer support, group or whole class activities. The computers are usually arranged around the walls and the individuals sit with their backs to each other. This is not the most promising layout to encourage communication. It suits an individual instruction approach but it is unlikely that in every session you will want to use only individual learning. This limits the benefits of e-learning and fails to achieve its full potential.

You are probably not free to move the computer equipment but you can organise the class to minimise this unpromising layout. Ask the learners to work in small groups (e.g. three people are normally able to work around a single computer) or move the chairs so that the class is not always facing the walls. Use the electronic whiteboard or a video projector to provide a different focus for the class. Each classroom will offer a different challenge but don't allow the physical layout to dictate your approach.

More important than the physical layout are the group dynamics and co-operation. During the first session, establish a class mailgroup so that everyone can communicate with each other between sessions. A useful way of introducing the topic is to ask the class to discuss what the rules (i.e. netiquette) for using the mailgroup should be. They are more likely to obey rules they have agreed on than ones imposed on them. If the college has standard rules then discuss those to achievement agreement. At this stage it is useful to explain what they can expect from you (e.g. you will answer all e-mails within 24 hours of receipt).

The college's virtual learning environment (VLE) can be a very useful resource as long as everyone understands what it can provide. At an early stage in the course the structure and benefits of the VLE needs to be shown to the group. One way of ensuring that the learners understand the VLE is to provide activities that involve using its resources (e.g. library catalogue, learning materials or other facilities).

Wireless computers offer considerable freedom to adjust the layout. The room can be divided into several areas and cross communication using e-mail can take place. This allows considerable flexibility.

Less structured environments

Community-based courses often take place in village halls, community centres and other locations that will have to be adapted for education and training purposes. It is possible to transport laptops, video projector and other resources but good preparation is vital. You need to be self-sufficient so it is important to:

- charge all the batteries – power points may not be adequate

- carry spare fuses, bulbs, leads and software

- check the facilities in advance so there are no surprises

- undertake a risk assessment of the room and routes

The limitations can offer some advantages, in that shared facilities (e.g. printers and Internet access) can be used to encourage collaboration.

Access to the Internet may be limited or even unavailable. It is a challenge to organise a class around a single connection and it certainly needs to be planned. However, a lot can be achieved and the response from learners who do not have access to ICT can be enormously beneficial.

Portable equipment, such as scanners, cameras, photocopiers, printers and projectors, now allow a wide range of technology to be made available in even the most remote locations. Hand held devices (e.g. Apple iphone) can be a powerful aid to learning.

Home

Communication technology enables learning to continue out of the classroom. Learners can continue to discuss issues with their colleagues between sessions and study at home. This does assume, of course, that the learners are interested and motivated to do so. Some will want to maintain a gap between home and college. If you want to take advantage of learning outside of the classroom, it is important to ensure that learners also wish to do so.

A useful approach is to ask groups of learners to undertake a joint assignment so that they are encouraged to communicate. However, you will often require that individual work is submitted so that it can be assessed. You will need to explain that they will work together until they submit, when it must then be a personal piece of work.

Interactive Whiteboard

Technology on its own will often contribute little to enriching the learning experience. It needs to be integrated with the learning objectives, effective pedagogy and planning. Electronic whiteboards are a good example. If they are used simply to present information then they are little different from many other forms of presentation technology. Little benefit will be gained if they are used like whiteboards and Overhead Projectors. They have the potential to provide a far more creative whole class discussion than is possible in more traditional ways. An electronic whiteboard can be used in the following ways:

- Enabling the integration of a wide range of resources into the classroom such as:

o websites

o videos

o learning objects

o open Educational Resources

o courseware

o notes and ideas captured at an earlier session

- Allowing learners to use the whiteboard to respond to questions, present the outcomes of tasks and to demonstrate their understanding

- Capturing the views of the whole group as a set of notes that can be distributed to the whole class; it can serve as a resource for other groups or can be shared with other tutors

- Giving the whole class feedback or briefing

- Creating (e.g. combining with mind mapping software to identify the relationships between different aspects of the issue) an interesting focus for activities

Whiteboards are a resource for both tutors and learners and should be used by both.

Video Conferencing

Video conferencing offers considerable potential to enhance learning by:

- Linking together two groups of learners:

- in different countries so that foreign languages can be practised

---

- in different colleges that are studying similar subjects

- Bringing an external speaker into the classroom

- Supporting a distant learner

- Creating a virtual visit

The effectiveness of video conferencing depends, like almost all e-learning approaches, on the degree of integration with the subject's curriculum. The opportunity to talk with natural speakers of a language you are studying is significant, although it does need to be carefully organised. If the technology is limited to individual webcams then the activities should be based on one-to-one interactions and activities. A version of speed dating could be used in which all students meet their colleagues one at a time for a few minutes. This can be fun and much can be achieved in a few minutes of focused discussion. It is essential that learners prepare for the event to maximise the opportunity.

The opportunities differ if the video conference is based on a large screen with cameras showing a whole room. This approach needs to be based around group-to-group interaction which requires a lot of planning and preparation. Activities can include:

- A debate with each group taking a different point of view on an issue

- Demonstrations

- Multiple site project

- Individual interaction with each student having an opportunity to speak to the other group although this can take a long time

A very different approach is to use video conferencing to import an external speaker into the classroom to talk on a relevant subject. This has been used widely in large companies and conferences.

Video conferencing provides the means to support distant learners, in essence, providing one-to-one tuition. There are other ways of communicating with learners but the power of vision should never be under-estimated.

One further possibility is the virtual visit. Learners could interact with a location (e.g. industrial site) so that they can see what happens in a place that is difficult to visit (e.g. power station, production line or farm).

All video conferencing is a form of team teaching in which the tutors needs to work closely with their colleagues at the other end of the link.

World Wide Web

The World Wide Web offers many benefits in the classroom. Two important ones are:

- information

- alternative learning environments

1. Information

There are various ways of using the enormous information resource that websites offer. However, it is vital that learners are aware that the quality of the information will vary between websites and they need to develop the skill of distinguishing between different sources. The key questions to ask you are:

1. Who published the information (e.g. government agency, university or individual)?

2. Is the author an appropriate person with respect to the information (e.g. university researcher)?

3. When was the information last up-dated?

4. How is the published information quality assured (e.g. online journal in which all papers are peer reviewed before they are published)?

5. Which websites have links to this information (e.g. government sites link to the website)?

It is often helpful to provide exercises that ask learners to compare different sources so as to develop these skills of information literacy.

One way of using the information provided by the World Wide Web is to design assignments that meet the course objectives by:

- providing lists of agreed sources so that learners are analysing the provided information rather than searching

- requiring distinct outcomes from the tasks

- setting deadlines for completion

Example

A Business Studies course may well ask students to analyse the trends in the availability of professional ICT staff to determine why there are skill shortages and then provide a list of sources such as:

- Online newspapers' business pages

- Individual organisation websites

- Professional bodies for staff or businesses

The alternative is to ask the students to find their own sources, which is reasonable if an objective of the course includes learning to search and to identify meaningful sources of information. A general search activity is often an effective initial exercise where you are seeking to encourage collaborative working or to introduce the students to each other.

2. Alternative learning environments

The World Wide Web offers a range of possibilities for alternative learning or teaching environments such as:

- blogs

- twitter

- wikis

- e-mail forums

- online applications (e.g. Goggle Docs)

These can all be used at the college or at other locations. Teaching often benefits from using a variety of methods and these sites allow for different types of interaction between learners and their tutors.

Creating a blog is an exciting way of encouraging individuals to reflect on their learning to produce a learning diary, it has the benefit that peers and tutors can contribute as well. Blogs can also be used for other purposes such as:

- a repository for useful links

- a means of peer support

- presenting frequently asked questions and their answers

A wiki is a powerful way of encouraging group co-operation and collaboration. It can bring a new dimension to a group task and encourage everyone to contribute. Most learners will happily add new information to a wiki but the task of editing an existing contribution can be quite daunting. It is good practice to provide the opportunity for everyone to add and edit contributions. A completely volunteer approach can lead to a long document being produced with few edits. In addition, wikis can also serve as:

- a store of content, with links to websites and papers that students have gathered in relation to a particular topic

- a way of providing support, with students posting questions that their peers or tutors can answer

E-mail forums are probably the most widely used method. They can be used for a variety of purposes that involve a group communicating, such as:

- mutual support – that is, ask a question and a peer will provide an answer

- discussion – to debate a topic (e.g. comment on a article)

- sharing learning experiences

- technical support – help with practical problems

- co-ordinating group activities

The key issue is of encouraging everyone to participate can be achieved in a variety of ways, including:

- asking all the students to introduce themselves

- asking each person to take a turn in facilitating discussion

- assessing contributions

No one particular way is guaranteed to be effective but the greatest success is likely to be achieved by integrating the forum into the course. If it is left as an added extra, it will often be poorly used.

Face-to-face discussion can usually help establish online forums quickly and effectively.

Open Educational Resources

The Open Education Resource movement, supported by the Hewlett Foundation, began several years ago, with universities providing online access to their course content. There is a growing group of sites around the world offering huge volumes of learning materials for any one to use but without any tutorial support from their hosts. The intention is that independent learners can have the benefit of high quality content. The Open University has established an open education resources site called OpenLearn. This will eventually provide access to 5% of all the university's materials.

The Learning and Skills Council commissioned a large volume of learning objects over several years. Known as NLN content, materials or learning objects, these materials are freely available to colleges in England and Wales.

There are several other repositories of content but these are often restricted to specific institutions, although the trend is to widen access. In addition, many national museums, libraries, The National Archive and art galleries offer access to large volumes of digital content. These resources are not specifically designed for learners but can be very useful.

Assessment

E-assessment is growing rapidly. Many awarding bodies now employ computer-based testing and in some cases these are provide online. There are numerous types of assessment but some extensively used approaches are:

1. Multi-choice questionnaires

A variety of tools are available that will allow you to create tests and quizzes based on asking learners to select the right answer from a list. These can be useful in providing learners with the means to self-assess. The key to designing the tests is to:

- present a range of questions that cover the curriculum being examined

- provide realistic choices of answer

- give feedback when a wrong answer is chosen (e.g. Wrong or a cross is of little value – provide a short explanation why the answer is incorrect that will develop the learners understanding)

- limit guesses so that it the test remains realistic

Self-assessments are a useful way of providing formative feedback to students.

2. Some tools will allow you to include other types of question such as dragging answers into gaps in the text, short open answers, selecting the true answers from alternatives and identifying items in a picture.

3. E-portfolios

Portfolios of evidence have been used in education and training for many years. E-portfolios are essentially the extension of the approach, providing additional benefits, such as the ability to:

- store multimedia evidence

- select specific items of evidence to match assessment criteria

- integrate links to online content

- add personal reflections to the evidence

- edit content

- store material for a lifetime

- search electronic content

In comparison, paper portfolios are frequently inflexible, large and difficult to maintain over a long period.

E-portfolios can either be online, enabling learners to gain access to them from anywhere, or they can be stored on an individual computer or memory stick.

There are several roles that an e-portfolio can, play such as:

- a store capable of holding a large collection of evidence of achievement and experience gathered over many years

- a specific sample of evidence to provide an electronic Curriculum Vitae, customised to meet the needs of a particular job

- a specific collection of evidence to demonstrate your competency or to meet the requirements of a qualification

There are various e-portfolio products available. Some have been designed for one or more of the above roles. However, it is perfectly possible to design your own, by creating a series of folders on Google Docs, Windows Live or another facility for storing content online.

Virtual Learning Environments (VLE)

A VLE can provide a wide range of information and services that can help learners. A significant advantage of a VLE is that it will allow them to gain access to these functions at college, at home or on the move. Some of the services and information that are typically available are:

- e-mail accounts for all students and tutors

- discussion forums so that learners can support each other between face-to-face session

- on-line self assessment

- course materials (e.g. handouts, course guides, reading lists and administration guidance)

- links to appropriate websites

- frequently asked questions (FAQs)

- individual records

- library catalogues

- links to selected websites

VLEs can provide support before, during and after a course. The list above is mainly linked to student needs during the course, but other functions that are useful before and after can include:

- Before – outlines of the course to help student decide if it is suitable for them

- After – providing extra learning materials so that learners can build on the course outcomes and offering access to the student's e-portfolio

A VLE is probably mostly used to provide copies of handouts and other course materials that are given out during sessions. This allows students who have missed a session to gain straightforward access to content and therefore to quickly catch up. However, it is often reported that by placing these materials online, student attendance will fall at face-to-face elements of the course. This is often the case if materials are made available in advance of the face-to-face sessions.

While the use of a VLE to provide access to materials and services can bring significant benefits, this does not realise the full potential of the platform. The key to achieving this potential is to encourage active learning. This can take several forms but group projects based on VLE discussion forums utilising resources located in the environment are one of the most straightforward.

The simple step of providing a VLE does not guarantee that it will be used or that learners will be able to locate the functions they need. It can often be useful at an early stage in a course to provide an exercise that requires students to explore the VLE and thus gain an understanding of how it can help them.

Summary

The key points of this chapter are that:

- e-learning and technology can be used in many ways to enhance teaching and learning (e.g. personal productivity, a focus for learning activities, creating learning materials, communication and assessment)

- e-learning can support the show, tell and do as well as memorise, understood and do approaches to teaching and training

- blending e-learning approaches with traditional teaching methods aims to gain the benefits of both approaches

- personal productivity can be enhanced through Office applications to produce high quality handouts and course materials and using presentation applications to create learning materials

- the organisation of the e-learning classroom needs to be carefully considered so as to create an effective learning environment (e.g. co-operation and mutual support).

- communication technology allows learning to continue out of the classroom, although some learners will want to achieve a study/life balance

- the use of interactive whiteboards needs to be integrated into the learning experience; they enable the presentation of a wide range of resources into the classroom and allow learners to participate by capturing their views and those of the whole group

- video conferencing has considerable potential to enhance learning by linking together two groups of learners, bringing an external speaker into the classroom, supporting a distant learner or by creating a virtual visit

- the World Wide Web has many benefits in the classroom - providing information and creating alternative learning environments

- the quality of the information will vary between websites and learners must be able to distinguish between different sources by considering who published the information, the appropriateness of author, when was the information last up-dated, how the information is quality assured and which websites have links to this information

- information activities need to be integrated into the course objectives

- the World Wide Web offers alternative learning or teaching environments (e.g. blogs, wikis, e-mail forums and online applications)

- a blog encourages individuals to reflect on their learning and can also be used for many purposes such as a repository, a source of peer support or a way of presenting frequently asked questions

- a wiki is a powerful way of encouraging group co-operation and collaboration; it can also serve as a store of content, links to websites and papers that students have gathered on a particular topic and a means of offering support

- e-mail forums can provide mutual support, discussion, sharing and co-ordination of group activities

- the Open Education Resource movement is growing rapidly and providing large volumes of learning materials

- e-assessment is expanding and many types are being used (e.g. multi-choice questionnaires, self-assessments and e-portfolios)

- e-portfolios provide the means to store multimedia evidence, match evidence to assessment criteria, link to online content, add personal reflections and edit or search content

- virtual learning environments (VLE) can provide a wide range of information and services (e.g. e-mail accounts, discussion forums, self assessment, course materials, and links to appropriate websites, Frequently Asked Questions (FAQs), individual records and library catalogues)

Chapter 6

Competent E-learning Tutor

A variety of e-learning standards are appropriate to tutors. They include:

- Lifelong Learning UK – this is the sector skills council for lifelong learning and is responsible for defining the standards required to teach or train in Further Education and Skills. It has standards for teaching and training that include using ICT (LLUK, 2005) as well as separate e-learning standards.

- The Learning Skills Network (2007) developed an e-CPD framework of units to assist with the professional development of staff working in the Further Education and Skills sector

- The Association of Learning Technology has developed a set of standards to support its certified membership scheme (CMALT) which is aimed at professional e-learning staff

These three developments provide the basis for this chapter which clarifies the skills and knowledge required for tutors to become competent users of e-learning. It is intended to help tutors identify what they need to study and develop. It is not intended to be an alternative occupational standard.

The following represent the skills and knowledge needed to employ e-learning effectively:

1. understanding of the nature of the subject (e.g. curriculum, areas that learners find difficult, ways that topics can be effectively presented to aid learning and the relationships between aspects of the subject)

2. understanding the needs of learners (e.g. preferred ways of learning, barriers they encounter and motivation to study)

3. technical skills and confidence in using ICT

4. supporting learners to develop their own technical and learning skills in order to benefit from e-learning

5. understanding the pedagogy of e-learning

6. facilitating, supporting and delivering individual, pairs, groups and whole class teaching or training when using ICT in the classroom or other face-to-face setting

7. facilitating, supporting and delivering online learning to individuals and groups

8. evaluating and judging the usefulness of e-learning materials and application

9. using ICT to create learning materials

10. using e-learning to provide formative and summative assessment

This may seem a formidable list but you do not need to be competent in all these aspects in order to make a start, and in using e-learning you will improve and extend your skills. There are also many areas of competence that relate to e-learning, such as research skills and information literacy.

Summary

The key points of this chapter are that:

- there is a variety of e-learning standards that are appropriate to tutors including standards and frameworks provided by Lifelong Learning UK, Learning Skills Network (2007) and Association of Learning Technology

- the skills and knowledge to employ e-learning includes both technological and pedagogical skills and understanding

- competence will improve with the use of e-learning

Chapter 7

Continuous Professional Development

Introduction

The requirement for continuous development of your skills and knowledge is now a normal part of most professions, and teaching and training is no exception. With e-learning this is a necessity because the subject is highly dynamic with new ideas, technologies and approaches becoming available all the time. It is essential to prioritise your development simply to maintain your understanding and skills.

Practical issues

Tutors need to be confident users of any e-learning technology that they employ. Confidence comes with familiarity. It is important that you give yourself time to use the technology and regular use will bring skill, confidence and effective use.

Example

You need to make regular use of an Electronic Whiteboard in order to develop the skills and understanding of how to integrate it effectively into sessions. Start modestly (e.g. show a useful website or ask your learners to do so) and gradually extend its use (e.g. to facilitate a whole class discussion) until you are confident that you understand it's potential. Once you can respond in a dynamic and spontaneous way, you will know that you are gaining the maximum benefit from the technology.

Professional Bodies

Most professional bodies for teachers and trainers now offer information and, in some cases, support in relation to e-learning. The two organisations below are important because they provide competency standards for practitioners with regard to e-learning.

The Association for Learning Technology (ALT) is for those interested in the use of learning technology. It has both individual and organisational members. It provides publications, conferences and good practice and has established a certificate and standards for Learning Technologists.

Lifelong learning UK (LLUK) is the sector skills council responsible for the development of teachers and trainers in lifelong learning. They have created standards for professional staff in relation to ICT and e-learning.

It is useful to compare your own skills and knowledge against the different standards in order to identify any gaps. This provides a straightforward way of assessing your own needs.

How to keep up to date

It is difficult to keep fully up-to-date with a continuously developing and changing subject like e-learning even if you were to devote all your time to the effort. However, you can keep yourself aware of developments through relatively simple actions such as:

- reading a national newspaper that has an educational edition because they will almost certainly report on new technology and its educational and training potential. Occasionally they have a special edition devoted e-learning.

- contacting organisations, such as BECTA, Future lab, JISC, NIACE and QIA who publish guides, briefings and reports on good practice and research. Their websites will also provide a doorway to a lot of detailed information.

- discussing options and practice with colleagues.

- participating in mailgroups provided by national, regional (e.g. regional Support Centres) and local organisations will let you discuss e-learning possibilities.

- enrolling in alerts service that will e-mail you about new developments in your chosen subject (e.g. Google Alerts - http://www.google.co.uk/alerts?hl=en).

- undertaking courses on e-learning for tutors, teachers and trainers. They vary in length, accreditation and content but do offer the opportunity to significantly develop yourself.

- exploring new technologies as they emerge to identify their potential to contribute to education and training.

- contributing to a blog and a wiki. Reflect on the experience. How did you feel and how could you use the experience to help your learners?

Professional reflection

There is a range of approaches to professional reflection but the one below is aimed at helping you develop your e-learning skills and knowledge.

After an experience of using technology or another similar activity you should consider:

1. How you would describe the experience in personal terms (e.g. how you felt?)

2. A critical review of the experience – what have you learnt? What would you consider as the key factors?

---

3. How would you relate the experience to your own teaching approach? What would you adopt? What would you reject? Consider why you have chosen to accept or reject the new ideas.

4. What improvements do you anticipate?

It is often useful to write down these reflections and review them later, perhaps when you are reflecting on the experience of using the new approach.

Summary

The key points of this chapter are that:

- Continuous Professional Development is essential for a rapidly developing and dynamic subject such as e-learning

- regular use of e-learning technology is essential to develop skills, use and confidence

- comparing your own skills and knowledge against the different standards provided by the Association for Learning Technology (ALT) and Lifelong Learning UK (LLUK) will identify areas for development

- in order to keep up to date you need to read the educational edition of a newspaper, study guides, briefings and reports on good practice and research; you should also discuss options and practice with colleagues, join e-learning mailgroups, subscribe to an alerts service and consider attending, exploring and evaluating new developments

- reflecting on your e-learning experiences will assist your development

Appendices

1. Sources of Information

Abilitynet – a charity that aims to help disabled people use ICT – http://www.abilitynet.org.uk/

ALT – Association for Learning Technology – professional association for learning technology http://www.alt.ac.uk/

BECTA – Government agency for e-learning covering schools and Further Education - http://www.becta.org.uk/

CIPD – Chartered Institute of Personnel and Development http://www.cipd.co.uk/default.cipd

Clarke, A (2006), Teaching Adults ICT Skills, Learning Matters

Disability Rights Commission - http://83.137.212.42/SiteArchive/drc_gb/default.aspx.html

Educause – non-profit organisation which encourages the use of technology in Higher Education https://www.educause.edu/node/720?time=1212165522 (accessed on 30th May)

Futurelab – new ways of using technology to enhance learning - http://www.futurelab.org.uk/

Go2Web20.net, Web 2.0 services and applications list, http://www.go2web20.net/ (accessed at 30 May 2008)

Hewlett Foundation - http://www.hewlett.org/Default.htm (accessed on 9th June 2008)

Internet Resources Newsletter - http://www.hw.ac.uk/ (accessed 22 June 2008)

JISC – Government organisation for e-learning covering Higher Education - http://www.jisc.ac.uk/

NIACE – National Institute for Adult Continuing Education – non-government organisation for widening participation http://www.niace.org.uk/

NLN – a large repository of learning objects designed for post compulsory education and training - http://www.nln.ac.uk/

Ofsted – the Office for Standards in Education responsible for inspecting post compulsory education and training http://www.ofsted.gov.uk/

Open Courseware Consortium - http://ocwconsortium.org/ (accessed 22 June 2008)

Open University, Open Educational Resources site, http://openlearn.open.ac.uk/ (accessed on 9th June 2008)

Portableapps.com, portable applications, http://portableapps.com/apps (accessed on 30 May 2008)

QIA Excellence Gateway – Quality Improvement Agency portal offering access to a wealth of information and resources for education and training - http://excellence.qia.org.uk/

Royal National Institute of Blind People (RNIB) Web Access - http://www.rnib.org.uk/xpedio/groups/public/documents/Code/public_rnib008789.hcsp

Royal National Institute for Deaf People (RNID) - http://www.rnid.org.uk/

RSC – Regional Support Centres - network of support centres covering English regions, Wales, Northern Ireland and Scotland - http://www.jisc.ac.uk/rsc

TechDis – Expert advice and guidance on accessibility in education and training - http://www.techdis.ac.uk/

Teachernet – many example lesson plans and other resources http://www.teachernet.gov.uk/

Webquest websites – http://webquest.org/index.php and http://www.aclresources.net/webquests/index.html

2. Tools

There is large and growing range of tools available that can help you deliver e-learning. Table 5 provides a list of some useful e-learning tools. Some of them are free while others are commercial products. They are simply some that I have found useful. There are many more. A list of thousands of tools relating to web 2.0 applications and services is available at Go2Web20.net (http://www.go2web20.net/). Portableapps.com (http://portableapps.com/apps) also provides applications that can be used from a memory stick or other portable device

Table 5   E-learning Tools

Tool	Description	Location
Articulate	E-learning tool to create learning materials and quizzes	http://www.articulate.com/
Audacity	Software to help you record and edit sounds (e.g. create podcasts)	http://audacity.sourceforge.net/
Blogger	Create blogs	https://www.blogger.com/start
Camtasia Studio	Create video of screens	http://www.techsmith.com/camtasia.asp
CourseLab	Course creation tool	http://www.courselab.com/

(Continue)

del.icio.us	Online bookmarking tool that allows you to share your sites with others	http://del.icio.us/
EclipseCrossword	Create crosswords	http://www. eclipsecrossword. com/
eXe	Web content authoring Tool	http://exelearning. org/
FreeMind	Mind mapping tool	http://freemind. sourceforge.net/wiki/ index.php/Main_ Page
GIMP	Photograph editing tool	http://www.gimp. org/
Google Docs	Online office applications that allow you store and access documents online	http://www.google. com/docs
Google Maps	Maps	http://maps.google. com/
Hot Potatoes	Applications to help you create tests and assessments	http://hotpot.uvic.ca/
LAME	Converts sound files into MP3 format Works with Audacity	http://lame. sourceforge.net/ index.php

(Continue)

Livejournal	Social networking tool	http://www.livejournal.com/
MindManager	Mind mapping tool	http://www.mindjet.com/uk/
Moodle	Virtual Learning Environment/Course Management	http://moodle.org/
OpenOffice	Free Office suite of application	http://www.openoffice.org/
PB Wiki	Wiki	http://pbwiki.com/
Picasa	Picture managing tool	http://picasa.google.com/
PhotoStory	Create slide shows	http://www.microsoft.com/windowsxp/using/digitalphotography/photostory/default.mspx
Second Life	Virtual World	http://secondlife.com/
Skype	Helps you make Internet Telephone calls	http://www.skype.com/intl/en-gb/
SnagIt	Screen capture tool	http://www.techsmith.com/screen-capture.asp

Thunder	Screenreader	http://www. screenreader.net/
Twitter	Communication tool	http://twitter.com/
Wikispaces	Wiki	http://www. wikispaces.com/
Wink	Create tutorial and presentations	http://www. debugmode.com/ wink/

3. Accessibility

Many learners have difficulties seeing, hearing and touching. The law requires that education and training organisations make reasonable adjustments to ensure that disabled learners are able to participate in activities. In essence, disabled learners should not be treated less favourably that their peers.

Equipment designed to help disabled learners is widely available and the Microsoft Windows operating system provides a range of functions. These include:

- keyboard – to help learners with difficulties of dexterity windows allows:

- you to press shift, ctrl and alt one at a time

- you to ignore accidentally pressing the same key twice

- a sound to be made if the caps, scroll or num lock keys are pressed

- sound – to help learners with hearing problems, a caption is displayed if speech or sounds are made by the computer system

- display – to help learners with sight problems:

- the display can be enlarged to maximise readability

- the mouse pointer can be adjusted to make it easier to see

- mouse – to help learners with dexterity problems, the mouse pointer can be controlled using the numbers pad

All these functions are available in the Control Panel (figure 4) within the Accessibility Options. There are also other useful functions available in other Control Panel options such as:

- display (settings option) – allows you to change the resolution and size of the icons

- keyboard

- mouse – provides a range of useful functions such as:

- making the mouse suitable for a left handed user

- adjusting the clicking rate

- adjusting dragging

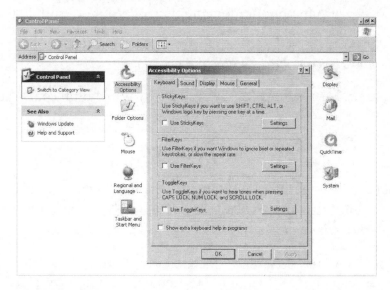

Figure 4 *Control Panel – Accessibility options*

In addition to the Control Panel options there are further functions in the Accessories Accessibility options (i.e. All programs menu, Accessories and Accessibility options). These are:

- Accessibility Wizard – this helps you to set the various options to help a disabled learner

- Magnifier – magnifies the display

- Narrator – reads displayed text aloud

- On screen keyboard – displays a keyboard so you can operate it with a pointer (e.g. mouse)

There are lots of adaptations and other approaches to assist disabled learners. It is often advisable to take advice from organisations such as:

1. Techdis - http://www.techdis.ac.uk/

2. Abilitynet - http://www.abilitynet.org.uk/

3. RNIB Web Access - http://www.rnib.org.uk/xpedio/ groups/public/documents/Code/public_rnib008789. hcsp

4. RNID - http://www.rnid.org.uk/

5. Microsoft Accessibility http://www.microsoft.com/enable/

Reference

ALI (2007), E-learning: fulfilling its potential in the adult learning sector, http://live.ofsted.gov.uk/publications/elearning/ (accessed on23 May 2008)

Association for Learning Technology, Certified Membership of Association for Learning Technology, http://www.alt.ac.uk/ (accessed on 22 June 2008)

BECTA (2007), Learning in the 21st century: The case for harnessing technology, BECTA, Coventry

CIPD (2006), E-learning: progress and prospects, http://www.cipd.co.uk/subjects/lrnanddev/elearning/elearnprog.htm (accessed on 23 May 2008)

Chickering, A.W. and Gamson, Z.F. (1987), Seven Principles for Good Practice in Undergraduate Education, American Association for Higher Education Bulletin, 39 (7), p. 3-7.

Clarke, A (2008), E-learning Skills, 2nd Edition, Palgrave McMillan

Clarke A, Reeve A, Essom, J, Scott J, Aldridge F, and Lindsay, K (2003), Adult and Community Learning Laptop Initiative Evaluation, NIACE

Golden, S, McCrone, T, Walker, M and Rudd, P (2006), Impact of E-learning in Further Education: Survey of Scale and Breadth, Research Report RR745, Department for Education and Skills

Hall Aitkin (2002), Evaluation of Pioneer and Pathfinder UK Online Centres: Follow up Study, RR36UK Research Report, DfES

Hartley, J. (1998), *Learning and Studying. A research perspective,* London: Routledge.

JISC (2004), Effective Practice with e-learning, a good practice guide in designing learning, JISC Development Group

JISC (2007), In their own words, Exploring the learners' perspective on e-learning, JISC e-learning programme

Kolb D (1984), Experiential Learning: Experience as the Source of Learning and Development. Prentice-Hall, Inc., Englewood Cliffs, N.J

LLUK (2005), e-learning standards, http://www.lluk.org/3089.htm (accessed 22June 2008)

LSN (2007), A professional development framework for e-learning, Learning and Skills Network

Northumberia University (2008), Exploring Tangible Benefits if e-learning – Does investment yield interest?, JISC Infonet

Twigg, C.A (2005), Increasing Success for Underserved Students, National Center for Academic Transformation